THE
HEARD
LEGACY

BY
CATHY SAGNIBENE APPLE
WITH
BARBARA KNIGHT JOHNSON

ISBN: 1461150442
ISBN-13: 9781461150442

This book is dedicated to
Kathryn Heard Craig with grateful appreciation
of her vision for the future and her generous bequests
benefitting the women of Collin County.

Kathryn Heard Craig

The Heard Legacy was funded in part by a grant from the Collin
County Historical Commission.

FORWARD: THE LEGACY LIVES ON

As Hilda Thomas Truett's great-granddaughter, I have always considered myself part of the Heard-Craig story. I have been lucky enough to be an Intern at the Heard-Craig Center for the summer of 2024. I am delighted with this opportunity due to my love of history, my love of my local community, McKinney, Texas, and I feel deeply close to my work through the connection to my family's history. I have always known that my great-grandmother, Hilda, was given educational opportunities (such as attaining a college degree) because of the support of the Craig's who homed and cared for her. This knowledge of their philanthropy has only expanded due to my time with the Center. My grandmother, Nancy Anne Truett Harris Powell, keeps the family legacy alive in the imagination and hearts of us, her grandchildren. Being here to experience where the stories took place has been wonderful.
~Ellie Austin

Every tour of the Heard-Craig Center boasts of the extraordinary leadership of Kathryn Heard-Craig and her cousin, Bessie. Customers' overwhelming acknowledgment reinforces the honor and accolades two very smart, visionary businesswomen. Today, we continue to paint a picture of these strong women who never veered from their core value of philanthropy and from their passion for helping others. It is with great pleasure that we re-establish this book to perpetuate our company's philanthropic mission. By doing so, the book pays homage to the many bright souls who have held a role in this historic women-led, Mckinney legacy, especially Ellie Austin, our intern.
~In gratitude, Dr. Karen Zupanic

PREFACE

This book is a narrative history of the J. S. and S. D. Heard families, their predecessors and descendants. Preserving the history of a family, the individuals and their lives, is a slow and deliberate task for the writer. Writers glean insights from glimpses into their subjects' day-to-day existence: in significant moments of happiness and joy, struggles and accomplishments, tragedies and deep sorrows.

Commissioned by the Heard-Craig trustees and executive director, it has been my privilege to peer into the lives of the Heard family through detailed research that was often a treasure hunt for new or not widely known information. In the process, original facts are confirmed or sometimes left undetermined by research, new information is discovered, and most importantly, a significant history was preserved.

The research process accessed many resources: notes, letters, documents and photos from the Heard-Craig family archives; files from a former president of Austin College in Sherman, Texas; local interviews; newspaper clippings; census and genealogy data; the Heard Natural Science Museum archives; and resources from the McKinney Public Library; and other historical sources.

We are greatly indebted to Austin College and their former president, the late John D. Moseley, for access to his collection of correspondence with Kathryn Heard Craig. Written during a time when letters were the common form of communication, her correspondence reveals an astute woman of immense business acumen with an in-depth understanding of the current events of her day. Documents from Dr. Moseley's collection also define the many philanthropic endeavors by the Heard families to the college.

Through the pages of this book may you experience the lives and the dedication of the John Spencer Heard and Stephen Dudley Heard families. Their influential yet unassuming lives were a strong and lasting force in McKinney's early days of business. The legacy of their support of cultural arts and education continues in the community today.

~ Cathy S. Apple

The Heard family is remembered for their philanthropy towards education and their beloved city of McKinney. Their legacy continues to benefit the citizens of North Texas through the Heard-Craig Center for the Arts and the Heard Natural Science Museum. The Heard-Craig Woman's Club Trust commissioned this book to honor the life and legacy of founder Kathryn Heard Craig known as Katie. She lived her life as her parents had taught her by giving generously to others. She could always be counted on to volunteer at her church (First Presbyterian), provide food for the sick, and to offer comfort to friends and strangers alike. Katie gave of her time, talent and pocketbook without any need for recognition or adulation. She was described by her friend Evelyn Searcy as "a sweet-spoken, genteel, loving person - always a lady."

Katie's cousin Bessie Heard, founder of the Heard Natural Science Museum, is the most well-known member of the family and has been widely written about. Miss Bess, as she was called, enjoyed the limelight (unlike her cousin) and reveled in being interviewed by newspapers. For this reason and due to her outgoing and outspoken personality she is long remembered and loved. Therefore, we have chosen to accentuate the highlights of her life while concentrating on the life of her dear friend and cousin, Katie. In commissioning this written account it is our purpose to celebrate the legacy of this generous family by sharing their story.

~ Barbara Johnson, Heard-Craig executive director

ARRIVAL IN AMERICA

The Heard family's journey to McKinney, Texas, began with Charles Heard Sr., who emigrated with his family from County Tyrone in Ireland to the Commonwealth of Virginia in 1675. The Scots-Irish family lore tells of his abrupt departure from Ireland after chasing the local clergy with a pitchfork in a dispute over tithing.

The rise from poor immigrants in the late 1600s to millionaires by 1900 was a hard, slow process. The Heard family made their way from Virginia to Wilkes County, Georgia, and then Van Buren, Arkansas. In 1862, a year into the Civil War, Charles Heard, Sr.'s descendants, Henrietta and Charles Clarkson Heard, were living in Van Buren and were desperate to escape the war, having had most of their possessions destroyed in skirmishes. Property owners, they had made their living in farming. Then married for twenty-two years, the family legend says they buried their gold for safekeeping and braved a long, difficult journey through lawless and dangerous country to Collin County, Texas.

They may have been encouraged by Henrietta's family, who had left Mississippi a decade earlier and settled near Melissa and Anna north of McKinney. Henrietta's father, Jonathan Allen, was one of the first settlers of Collin County and the first judge to preside at the county seat, in then Old Buckner (now off U.S. Highway 380 west of McKinney). According to his obituary, Allen also practiced medicine, which he had learned by reading "doctor's books."

The family was accompanied by freed slaves and brought few belongings according to grandson Arthur Field Heard. There were ten children born to the Heards and two died as infants. Their sons John and

James were serving in the Confederate Army at the time of the move, so the couple brought six children to Texas: Clark, Stephen, Florence, Charles, Anna, and William. They set up the family's first business at the old City Hotel, known around town as "the boarding house," at Virginia and Wood Streets.

A FATEFUL JOURNEY

Charles Clarkson Heard was brutally murdered at age fifty-two in 1866 when he returned to Arkansas to recover the family gold and to sell some property. According to accounts in the Dallas Herald and the McKinney Messenger, Heard and two companions had collected about $1,500 while in Fort Smith, Arkansas. They were returning home when they were joined by two men who offered to care for their horses and do other work in exchange for transportation to Texas. When they were thirty-six miles beyond Boggy Depot in the Choctaw Nation (present-day Atoka County, Oklahoma), the hired men murdered the three McKinney men with an axe and set the bodies afire. They then fled with the money, two mules and Mr. Heard's wagon.

The men separated near the Red River where one of them stopped to see his wife. The other man made his way to Bonham, Texas, where he was arrested for an earlier offense. While in custody his complicity in the murders was discovered and he was burned to death by enraged citizens in Bonham.

Newspaper accounts stated that his companion in crime, fearing a similar fate, hired a guide for $50 to accompany him to Fort Smith, Arkansas. The guide betrayed him by handing him over to a group of men from Fannin County who were pursuing him. When he tried to escape, he was shot to death.

Charles Heard's body was returned to McKinney and buried at Pecan Grove Cemetery beside his wife, Henrietta. Mrs. Heard had died in 1864, just two years after they ar- rived in McKinney. The Heard's son James died at twenty-one fighting in the Civil War under Brigadier

General W. L. Cabell, a four-time former mayor of McKinney. Their son William left for California and was never heard from again.

The Heard's eldest son, John Spencer, who had rejoined the family in McKinney after the war, would devote the next decades to raising his siblings.

THE
HEARD LEGACY BEGINS:
JOHN & STEPHEN

By 1900, two Heard brothers, John Spencer and Stephen Dudley, had influenced nearly every aspect of business and industry in McKinney, Texas – in a very real sense, the city flourished with and because of the Heards. But their touch extended beyond business expertise: again and again, acquaintances and associates talk about the Heard generosity and their support for education and other endeavors, much of which is still visible today.

JOHN SPENCER HEARD (1841 - 1933)
RACHEL CAROLINE WILSON HEARD (1855 - 1934)

John Spencer Heard
1885 wedding portrait

Rachel Caroline Wilson Heard
1885 wedding portrait

John Spencer Heard was born in Fayetteville, Washington County, Arkansas, and was a Civil War veteran by the time he arrived in McKinney. He served in the Frontier Guard in Van Buren, Arkansas, as clerk and quartermaster for Brown's Company, Third Regular Arkansas Troop. After the battle of Oak Hill, John's company became part of the Twenty-Second Regiment, Arkansas infantry under the command of Colonel Rector. John fought in many battles, and was captured at the battle of Helena, Arkansas. He was released as part of a prisoner exchange, and served with the Confederate forces until General Robert E. Lee surrendered at Appomattox.

John married Rachel Caroline Wilson of Mississippi in 1885. Rachel was born and raised on her father's plantation in Lexington, Holmes County, Mississippi, and had moved with her family to a ranch in Collinsville, Texas. Her father, William Henry Wilson, was a soldier in the Confederate Army. He had been a large slaveholder in Mississippi before he moved with his wife, Elisabeth Campbell Pickens Wilson, and their ten children to Grayson County, Texas. Rachel and her older sisters attended Presbyterian Synodical College in Florence, Alabama.

Rachel was described as a lady of dignity, grace, and gentleness of manner. She was a talented artist who taught her daughters the skills that every young woman of the time should know. She patiently taught them china painting, quilting, and other handwork. She was an accomplished musician and an avid gardener who grew rare flowers in her two greenhouses. Her obituary noted: "Her sympathetic heart and helpful hand were extended in liberal but unostentatious ways to the deserving in times of sorrow and need."

Rachel and John's first home was a large Victorian at the corner of Virginia and Church Streets. The house had spacious rooms, tall ceilings, breezy porches, and beautiful wood- work. The couple had five daughters, Bessie (1886 – 1988), Nina (1888 - 1972), Grace (1889 - 1890), Laura (1893 - 1971), and Imogene (1897 - 1898).

John Heard Home

Nina C Bessie Heard (Nina, left)

John, Laura & Rachel Heard

Imogene Heard

John Heard took great pride in the development of the city of McKinney, its industries and its businesses. He was looked upon as one of the most astute businessmen in the state due to his many successful ventures. He was an organizer and director of the Collin County National Bank, and instrumental in the success of the Texas Cotton Mill, McKinney Compress, McKinney Ice & Coal, Fidelity Insurance Company, Gulf Fire Insurance Company, and numerous fire, life, and casualty companies. His daughter Bess said that his business diversification was one of the secrets of his great success.

One of his major accomplishments was establishing a mass transportation system with the Interurban, officially called the North Texas Traction Company. In 1903, John Heard and J. F. Strickland, signed papers in Boston to build an electric rail line that eventually would connect Sherman to Waco. The initial expense of equipment, powerhouse machinery, five substations, and fifteen cars purchased in 1906 was $250,000. It began regular operation on July 1, 1908, and showed a net profit on its earnings in the first quarter. The line was expanded with the purchase of the Sherman-Denison Interurban line. The Interurban was a marvel of mass transit for its day, but the growing popularity of automobiles led to it making its last run on December 31, 1948.

John was a man with a sense of humor, and often said that the Interurban was his "most expensive investment" because his wife and daughters would often board the Interurban to Dallas for a day of shopping.

He was a devoted family man who believed strongly in the importance of education. He served on the city's first school board in 1881 and joined a group of citizens that organized a local boarding school called the McKinney Collegiate Institute. John is credited with naming College Street to honor the establishment of the local college.

John Heard

Rachel Heard

John Heard

Rachel Heard

Rachel and John S. Heard were married forty-nine years before his death on November 22, 1933. Her decline in health began soon after this, and she died less than eleven months later on October 2, 1934.

STEPHEN DUDLEY HEARD (1847 - 1926)
LILLIE DALE SNAPP HEARD (1854 - 1932

Stephen Dudley Heard 1879 wedding portrait

Stephen Dudley Heard was born in Crawford County, Arkansas, the fourth of ten Heard children. He attended private schools in Van Buren, Arkansas, and Cane Hill College in Cane Hill, Washington County, Arkansas. When he arrived in McKinney at sixteen, he attended local schools and later Carlton College in Bonham, where families paid tuition in goods or labor and no student was ever turned away. He attended Bastrop Military Institute, graduating in 1865. When he returned to McKinney, he joined his older brother, John, in business as livestock traders. They would remain business partners and best friends for the rest of their lives.

Lillie Dale Snapp Heard 1879 wedding portrait

Lillie Dale Snapp, the daughter of Methodist preacher and attorney William Dulaney Snapp and Seraphina Catherine (Kate) Jackson Dulaney Snapp was born in Walnut Grove, Sullivan County, Tennessee. The Rev. Snapp was not related to the Dulaney family, but he admired them; and added Dulaney as his middle name. When he married Kate he became a Dulaney family member through the marriage.

Their daughter Lillie was just three in 1857 when the family moved to McKinney from Bristol, Tennessee in a U.S. mail coach purchased for the trip. The coach was considered to be the height of luxury at the time. They traveled west through Memphis, and then boarded a boat that carried the coach and their belongings down the Mississippi River to New Orleans. The family took the Red River to Jefferson and then traveled over land to Collin County. The journey took more than two months.

The Rev. William Dulaney Snapp

The Rev. Snapp played a prominent role in early McKinney as one of the first mayors. He contracted with the government for mail delivery from Old Mantua (near Van Alstyne) to Denton and later from McKinney to Denton, in the coach he had purchased for his family's trip to Texas. He served two years in the Confederate Army, contracted a lung ailment and died in 1864. Although his coach and horses continued to deliver the mail, the U.S. government refused to pay his wife because he had served in the Confederate Army.

Kate Dulaney Snapp (first row, right)

Kate Snapp was an accomplished seamstress who kept her daughters and son, William Joseph, well dressed. Her granddaughter, Katie Heard Craig, remembered her grandmother telling her how she had made a set of red slippers for her daughters, Lillie and Bonna De Ella, from the velvet of her husband's vest.

The Snapp children attended Muse Academy on North Waddill Street in the 1860s. Lillie continued her education with private tutors and at Mt. Pleasant High School in McKinney. She joined the First Presbyterian Church soon after it was organized, taught Bible study, and remained a member for more than fifty-five years.

Stephen Dudley Heard and Lillie Dale Snapp were married on June 26, 1879. They were the parents of three children though their first son died shortly after his birth in 1880. Their second son, Fredric Dulaney (Dudley) Heard, was born on January 12, 1882, and daughter Kathryn, known by her nickname Katie, was born May 23, 1884.

Stephen & Lillie Heard's first home (Maid, Fred, Lillie)

Katie wrote about her parents, Stephen and Lillie Heard, for the Austin College Archives, describing them in a letter to college president Dr. W. B. Guerrant:

I wish you might have known personally my father and mother, so I shall try to give you a little more intimate view of their lives as their daughter knew them. My father was six feet tall, had broad shoulders and a very erect posture even at the age of seventy-eight.

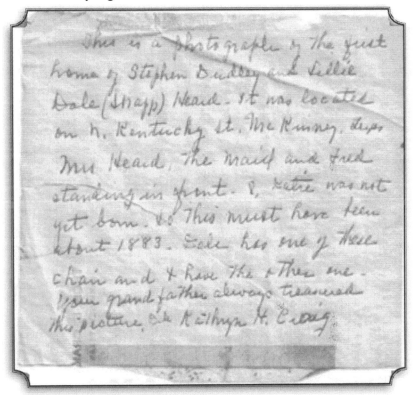

Note from her Aunt Katie to Dale Heard on the back of the first home photo

He was a man of few words and a dry wit. His word was as good as his bond and he was a true friend. My mother though never physically robust was a tower of strength in her family upon whom all of us leaned heavily. She had a sunny disposition and no matter how dark an outlook might be, she could always find a silver lining in the cloud, by her cheerfulness and wise council bring courage, and hope to others. My parents were devoted to each other through a wedded life of forty-seven years. Thinking and planning for the good and happiness of their children, they thought of others too and my mother kept the little poem "Others" pinned in her Bible. Long before the days of Rotary (Club) they lived by the motto "Service before Self" often extending helping hands, encouragement or council as the need and opportunity arose. Theirs was a true partnership; they did things together, consulting each other about family, church and community affairs. My father often asked mother's advice about business matters and gave her much credit for whatever success he may have had.

Stephen D. Heard had a lifelong interest in farming, enjoying the friendship of his tenants and personally supervising the cultivation of his farms and the clearing of land. He was a noted horseman with a great interest in harness racing.

At the turn of the century (1900), Stephen and Lillie Heard built their home, which still stands today as a testament to time and beauty. The home was built on property that was owned jointly by Stephen and John and was once a stagecoach stop on the Bonham, Texas line. John generously deeded his share of the property for $5 so that Stephen and Lillie could build their dream home. In this home, now known as the Heard-Craig House, they shared the joy of the birth of their grandchildren; the wedding of their only daughter, Katie; and the untimely funerals of their son, Fred, and grandson, Stephen.

Stephen Dudley Heard died September 11, 1926 at age 78. The notice in the McKinney Courier-Gazette says, "Probably no man ever lived in our city who built more in a business and industrial way than Stephen Dudley Heard."

His obituary described him as a loving husband and father, and "unusually successful as a businessman." It continued:

He was faithful as a friend and his character, stability and trustworthiness were above reproach. He did not

Heard Home 1900

Stephen Heard Home 1930s

Stephen Heard Home 1930s

disappoint his friends; but on the contrary he went beyond their expectations. He was a man of commanding physique and personality whose very presence and quiet, unobtrusive personality seemed to radiate stability and confidence throughout his long, busy and useful career. But in the intimacy of his family circle his character shone most resplendently. Never did a home possess more love and faith and unselfishness than did his as a husband and father. He was a just man and oppressed no one. He was charitable and extended many substantial favors in an unostentatious way to tide numerous men over the problems of life. He was always willing to assist in worthy causes.

Mayor Tom W. Perkins called Heard a giant in McKinney business and industry. "Being a man of quiet nature and reserved he did not push himself upon the public, although the public often sought his advice, counsel and influence. Wise in thought, discretionary in action, he was firm and decisive," wrote Perkins. "Out of respect to his memory, and for the wonderful work and accomplishments for our great state, county and city, I kindly and courteously ask that all business institutions of our city close from 3 to 4 p.m. today, the hour of the funeral of the city's beloved friend and business and industrial builder."

Besides his own holdings, Stephen was a director, organizer, or stockholder in the businesses that were the economic engine of McKinney and North Texas: cotton mills, banks, power and light companies, insurance agencies, the telegraph and telephone, and many more. He owned considerable real estate in McKinney, as well as in other parts of Texas and in Oklahoma. He was one of the organizers, directors and officials of many businesses, including: the McKinney Compress Company, the McKinney Cotton Oil Mill, Collin County Mill and Elevator Company, Burrus Mill and Elevator Company of Fort

Worth, Bonded Warehouse Company, Collin County National Bank, McKinney Ice & Coal Company and Farmer's Texas Cotton Mill in McKinney. According to the Collin County Historical Commission, the Texas Cotton Mill Company became one of only two mills west of the Mississippi River that manufactured dyed-print cloth. As one of the founders of the Cotton Compress Company of McKinney, Stephen gradually bought up all the outstanding stock until he and his son-in-law, Thomas Edgar Craig, owned the entire plant.

Lillie Heard passed away on February 12, 1932, at the age of seventy-eight. Her obituary stated that "she passed as she had lived, thinking of others." Lillie's granddaughter, Dale, wrote to her in 1928 expressing her thoughts and those of others by saying, "My grandmother [Lillie] possesses

Stephan Dudley Heard

every virtue - honor, fortitude, integrity, love, charity, gentleness, unselfishness, self-control, piety, duty, sweetness and everything else that is good. Her character is lovely and beautiful, and scholars might envy her mind and intelligence. Her life has been a series of beautiful and unselfish deeds."

Lillie Heard

J.S. AND S.D. HEARD
MERCANTILE

John and Stephen Heard began their business partnership soon after Stephen graduated from the military institute in 1865. The 1870 U.S. Census reported them as livestock traders, buying and selling horses, mules, and cattle. When they had amassed a large herd, the brothers would drive the herd to market. That year, John had personal property valued at $2,500 and real estate valued at $2,500. Stephen had personal property holdings valued at $2,500 and $1,000 in real estate.

J. S. & S. D. Heard Mercantile - Circa 1870
(West side of McKinney Square)

They expanded their partnership into the retail business when they opened the J. S. & S. D. Heard Mercantile in downtown McKinney, and remained merchants for nearly twenty-five years. Their store offered a variety of necessities including farm implements and tools, vehicles, harnesses, groceries, and fine, hand-sewn saddles.

Within a short period, the Heard brothers amassed a fortune of $5,000. At this time in Texas history, the security of banks was questionable so the brothers kept their cash at the mercantile in what was considered the only secure safe in town. They shared the use of their safe with friends and business associates in the late 1860s until the unthinkable happened: it was robbed. The Heard brothers proved their integrity by selling their own properties to repay their friend's losses. John and Stephen found themselves back to their financial beginnings with the prospect of starting over again. Their good reputations made it possible to borrow money to begin again. Bessie Heard, John's daughter, said many years later that her family knew who had robbed the safe, but that his identity was never revealed as "he was too high up to be touched."

The J. S. & S. D. Heard Mercantile building and all of the west side of the downtown square burned on January 21, 1887. John and Stephen's brother, Charlie, clerked for them and lived above the store. He lost all of his possessions in the fire along with $1,000 that was stored in a trunk. The Heard building burned again in 1924, and the brick structure at 107 N. Kentucky that replaced it in 1925 is still standing and in use as a restaurant and hotel. The building façade still holds a carved stone at the top with the name Heard inscribed.

The brothers' fortunes and many others' began to rise once North Texas became home to "King Cotton" and the railroad. The Heards played a part in bringing the Houston & Texas Central Railroad to McKinney, providing local farmers access to world markets. Railroad workers would stay at the Heard family's first business, the old City Hotel. The square at harvest time was packed with horse and mule drawn wagons loaded with cotton bales. By 1890, nearly fifty thousand bales of cotton a year were produced in the county. Each fall, local merchants donated prize money for the first farmers to arrive downtown with cotton for baling. Cotton would make Collin County one of the richest in the nation per capita.

The Heard brothers established a cottonseed oil mill in 1892 that revolutionized the industry in McKinney. Before the mill, cottonseed was little more than a nuisance, discarded as an unusable byproduct that turned the ditches a snowy white. The new mill with forty employees produced three hundred thousand gallons of oil in 1898, with cottonseed bringing $12 a ton.

THE HEARD OPERA HOUSE

In December 1884, the Heards were staging an inaugural ball to open the Heard Opera House. Bessie Heard later said that the inspiration for the opera house came from her mother's love of opera. McKinney historian Bill Haynes wrote in the December 2001 edition of The McKinney News, "It is appropriate that this first event at the Heard Opera House reported in a McKinney newspaper was a ball given during the Christmas holiday season, for the Opera House was to be at the center of the city's Christmas celebrations for the next quarter of a century."

Opera House Newspaper Advertisement

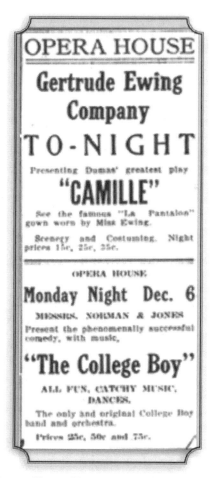

Opera House Newspaper Advertisement

Haynes referenced an article in the McKinney Democrat describing the new building "...on the first floor is a set of elegant business rooms, and above a handsome opera room one hundred by sixty feet. The front of the stage is paneled in red velvet, with a circle overhead which is to bear a lone star. The front curtain bears, in a perfect perspective, a sea- shore and a landscape with mountains. Cards with names of principal city businesses surround the stage. When the people of McKinney are called together at Heard Opera, a first class entertainment may always be looked for." An entry from the McKinney Democrat on January 8, 1885, mentions that "the skating rink in the Heard's Opera House opened last Tuesday night."

The opera house staged musical comedies at Christmas time throughout the 1890s. By 1904, Haynes writes, "the name had changed to McKinney Opera House, and a new curtain depicted Golden Gate Harbor. By 1907, the Opera House faced strong competition from a little theater on North Kentucky Street that specialized in one and two reel moving pictures. Competition was getting fierce; it was an exciting time. Moving pictures were becoming popular and vaudeville was dying."

The last event staged in the Opera House was the annual Collin County Oratorical Contest on March 26, 1910. The McKinney Daily Courier-Gazette ran an article reporting that this was "one of the largest and most enthusiastic audiences ever gathered in the Opera House. Words can hardly express the scene of unrestrained enthusiasm at the Opera House Saturday night when fourteen students from various schools over the county competed before a vast throng for the cash prizes amounting to $180."

Two days later, fire broke out on the east end of the stage and the opera house burned. The Heard brothers chose to not rebuild. The McKinney Daily Courier-Gazette ran an article on November 28, 1910, stating, "It was generally hoped by the entire people of the city, that they [the Heards] would repair the building, and make the house bigger and more elaborate than in the past. The opera house will be converted into a business house, hence McKinney, the largest town in all Texas without a place of amusement, will in the future be entirely without an opera house, and the people will have no place to go for amusements or first class shows. There is 'oodles' of money in McKinney, but it seems none to build a first class 'playhouse' with."

THE NEXT GENERATION

John, Rachel, Stephen and Lillie Heard were devoted parents instilling in their children a love of community and service to others. Living in homes that shared backyards they were not only family and business partners, but best friends throughout their lives. Their children honored their parent's legacy and lived as their parents would have wished, becoming successful in business and as philanthropists.

FREDRIC DUDLEY HEARD (1882 – 1910)
REMBERT ELIZABETH SMITH HEARD (1879 – 1943)

Stephen and Lillie Heard's son, Fredrick Dulaney Heard, was born in 1882. When he was fifteen he had his middle name legally changed to Dudley in honor of his father. Fred attended Austin College in Sherman, Texas, in 1897 and later transferred to Princeton University. His father brought him home and put him to work, it was said, after he started majoring in horse racing and parties. Coaching at McKinney Collegiate Institute was Fred's first job and it was there he met his future wife, Rembert Elizabeth Smith. Houston natives and graduates of St. Mary's College, Rembert and her sister, Georgie, both taught at the school.

With only two years difference in age, Fred and his sister, Katie, were close friends and confidants. He wrote to her about his marriage plans in a letter dated January 28, 1905, while she was attending Mary Baldwin College:

Fred Heard

Fred Heard Princeton University (1st Row, 1st on left)

Fred Heard

Charcoal Drawing by Fred Heard

There is no news at all and I suppose the little bird has told you all of the news about Miss Smith, you asked her name it is Rembert, now don't say you don't think it is pretty for I do. Miss Smith says that she will marry me on condition that you give Kid [Katie's horse] to her and I know that you would not spoil all my future happiness by refusing to so do would you? We are going to write to you a joint letter some time in the near future so don't be surprised.

Fred and Rembert were married on June 7, 1905, at St. Andrew's Episcopal Parish in Fort Worth. Their wedding began at 9 a.m. and the couple arrived by train in McKinney at 1:15 p.m. The next evening Stephen and Lillie hosted two-hundred guests at their McKinney home for a reception.

The young couple lived a block west of Fred's parents in a two-story frame house with turn-of-the-century architecture. They had two children, both of whom were born in Fred's parent's home, now known as the Heard-Craig House at 205 West Hunt Street.

Fred Heard
Katie Heard's 1910 Wedding

Rembert Smith Heard Katie Heard's 1910 Wedding

Fred & Rembert with Friends
(Top Row, l: Fred, Rembert)

Fred was manager and part owner for four years of the McKinney Compress Company established by his father, and was active in the family's investment/real estate business, Collin County Abstract Company. He served two years as an alderman on the McKinney City Council in the early 1900s. Fred and businessman Harry White were partners in the automotive firm Heard & White.

The McKinney Daily Courier-Gazette ran a story on May 11, 1910, reporting an automobile accident occurring when a car driven by Fred with his family and another couple crashed after a tire blew out. The story said that:

> Mr. Heard tried to shut off the Presto light, but could not. He crawled under the car and rescued his little girl, carrying her several feet away. In a moment the gasoline tank caught fire and reduced the handsome car, a few moments before a thing of speed and power, to a mass of wreckage practically worthless. All the party congratulated themselves and each

other that they escaped with minor injuries, where but for the coolness and promptness of action of Mr. Heard they might have lost their lives, especially the ladies and children. To the credit of the ladies, be it said, there was no excitement or screaming. They acted as promptly and coolly as the men.

Fred traveled to St. Louis and Memphis in early December 1910 to purchase machinery for the McKinney Compress Company. Two weeks later on December 14, he died in Memphis of heart failure, with alcoholism considered as the contributing factor. The McKinney Elks Lodge waited at the train station for Fred's body, and provided an escort via a special car on the Interurban line.

Services were held at the home of his parents, Stephen and Lillie Heard. Fred and Rembert's daughter, Kathryn Dale Heard (1906 – 1986), known as Dale, was four years old; and their son, Stephen Dudley Heard, Jr. (1907 – 1915), named after his grandfather, was 3. Dale later spoke of that day remembering their nurse holding them on the porch railing as they looked toward their grandparents' home while the community gathered for her father's funeral.

Five years after Fred's death, his son, Stephen, died of scarlet fever in 1915 at age eight. This funeral was also at the home of Stephen and Lillie Heard. Dale Heard wrote many years later that after the tragedy of her brother's death and her father's five years earlier that her mother desperately felt the need to get away and embarked with Dale on a cruise around the world. Dale said that all she wanted for herself at that terrible time was to be with her grandparents in their home where she had always felt safe.

Dale Heard received a bachelor of arts degree in 1923 from Texas Presbyterian College in Milford. In the fall of 1924, she enrolled at Southern Methodist University in Dallas and graduated in 1927 with a bachelor of arts degree.

Dale C Stephen Jr. 1908

Dale & Stephen Jr. at Home

Dale
Ring Bearer in Aunt Katie's 1910 Wedding

Stephen Jr.
Dressed for Aunt Katie's 1910 Wedding

Dale, Age 8 & Stephen Jr., Age 7

Birthday Party at their Grandparents' Home
Dale (5th from right) Stephen Jr. (15th from right)

A world traveler, artist, and aspiring screenwriter, she lived in Hollywood and eventually built a home in Los Angeles though she always kept a home in Dallas.

After the death of her mother in 1943, Dale traveled between Los Angeles and Dallas often. She spent a great deal of time in McKinney with her Aunt Katie, whom she affectionately called "Diddy."

When Dale accepted Dallas businessman Joe O. Lambert's marriage proposal in 1946 she decided to put her home in California up for lease. A telegram to Dale from a Los Angeles Realtor stated that the actor, Danny Kaye, was interested in renting her home and that he was considered to be a good renter.

Dale with her grandmother, Lillie Dale Heard

Dale

Dale

Dale (seated) & Friend

Dale (left) in Miami 1937

Dale in Hollywood

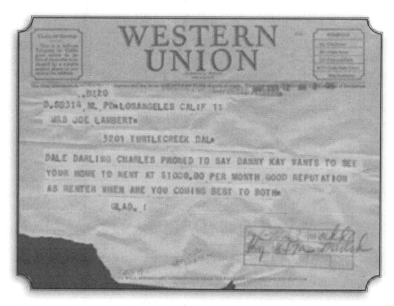

telegram

Dale &Joe lambert (Dale, left, seated by Joe)

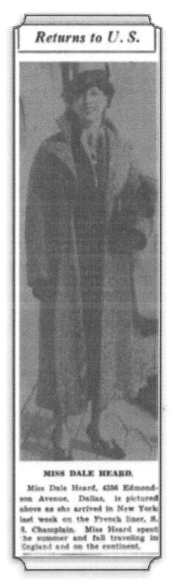

Returns to U. S.

MISS DALE HEARD.

Miss Dale Heard, 4356 Edmondson Avenue, Dallas, is pictured above as she arrived in New York last week on the French liner, S. S. Champlain. Miss Heard spent the summer and fall traveling in England and on the continent.

This clipping reads "Miss Dale Heard, 4356 Edmondson Avenue. Dallas, is pictured above as she arrived in New York last week on the French liner, S.S Champlain. Miss Heard spent the summer and fall traveling in England and no the continent

Watercolor Painted by Dale in Ireland

Dale's primary residence was in the upscale community of Highland Park in Dallas where she enjoyed the full and active life of a socialite. Her marriage to Lambert was short- lived and ended in 1948. She never remarried and died in Dallas in 1986 at the age of 80.

KATHRYN (KATIE) FLORENCE HEARD CRAIG (1884–1970)

Katie lived her life by the Bible verse, Luke 12:48, "For unto whomsoever much is given, of him shall be much required; ..." Her parents taught her this verse in early childhood and she let it guide her life and philanthropy.

She grew up surrounded by strong proponents of education, and gained business expertise from her father. She learned the traditional Southern female arts of painting, piano and needlework. By the age of eight, she was an accomplished artist of watercolor and pastel; and her love of art would be the great passion of her life.

Katie, Age 5

Katie, Age 7

Watercolor by Katie, Age 8

Watercolor by Katie, Age 12

Katie & Friends (Katie -1st from right)

Katie

Katie

Katie & Friends (Katie, 2nd from left)

After attending McKinney Collegiate Institute, Katie and her cousins Bessie and Nina Heard traveled to Staunton, Virginia, in 1902 to attend Mary Baldwin Seminary for Girls (now Mary Baldwin College). The cousins were roommates and shared many adventures during their three years at the school before returning to their homes in McKinney.

Katie played on the Black Diamonds basketball team, enjoyed acting in theatre productions and was dorm president during her four years at Mary Baldwin. She was awarded the "Golden Report" for a grade average of 90 or above.

In 1907, Katie met Thomas Edgar "Tec" Craig, who would become her husband. Tec, an electrical engineer, was working as a supervisor on the Interurban line near McKinney when he took the opportunity to look up his friend from Austin College, Fred Heard. Tec was smitten upon meeting Katie, but

Margaret Erwin's Art Studio
(l to R: Katie, Mattie Houston, Bessie Heard)

soon moved to Corpus Christi where he was hired as manager of the Peoples Electric Light and Power Company. The couple corresponded through postcards and were engaged on March 29, 1909. Katie treasured the postcards and saved all of them which were dated from 1907 to 1910.

Three years after they met, Katie, age 26, and Tec, age 35, began a marriage that would last forty-seven years. On November 2, 1910, the Heard family home was decorated with pink and white chrysanthemums for their wedding which was attended by two hundred guests.

Katie descended the oak staircase in white satin trimmed with lace and pearls, her veil held in place by lilies of the valley. She wore a locket set in pearls, rubies, and diamonds - her wedding present from Tec. Her cousin Bessie Heard and friend Georgie Smith were bridesmaids; sister-in-law, Rembert Smith Heard, was matron of honor and her niece, Dale Heard,

Mary Baldwin Seminary
(1st Row, left to Right: Cousins Nina, Katie, Bessie)

Bessie & Katie at Mary Baldwin

Katie 1909

was ring bearer and carried the ring in a single white chrysanthemum.
The couple stood beneath an arch decorated with flowers and blue lights
in the library. They left for their honeymoon on the 6:55 p.m. train to
Houston and later visited Galveston and San Antonio. They made their
home in Corpus Christi where they were given a large welcoming
reception by Tec's friends when they returned from their honeymoon.

After the death of Katie's brother, Fred, and with the
encouragement of her parents, Katie and Tec returned to McKinney in
1911. Her parents helped them build a home of their own that they
called, "The Honeymoon Cottage," located at the corner of Lamar and
Church Streets a short distance from her parents. The couple designed
the home to

Lillie, Stephen C Katie at Seven Falls, Colorado

minimize housecleaning and installed a central vacuum system. After Katie's father, Stephen Heard, died in 1926, they donated the "The Honeymoon Cottage" to the First Presbyterian Church; and moved into her parents' home with her mother, Lillie.

Kathryn Heard 1910 Bridal Portrait

Thomas Edgar Craig 1910 Wedding Portrait

Katie & Tec 1911

Honeymoon Cottage

THOMAS EDGAR CRAIG
"TEC" (1875 – 1957)

   Thomas Edgar Craig's family moved to Texas from Mississippi. His mother, Ella Virginia Owens married James Leroy Craig and the couple settled in Sulphur Springs. Son Thomas Edgar Craig was born on March 3, 1875, followed by the birth of two more sons: James Dunbar Watt Craig in 1885 and Paul Kerr Craig in 1892.

Thomas Edgar Craig

Ella Virginia Owens Craig

James Leroy Craig

Tec's family moved to Sherman, Texas when he reached college age in order for him to attend Austin College. He was one of four graduates of the class of 1898 and later described those years as his "most treasured memories from his college days." In a letter to the Sherman Chamber of Commerce during his business career, he notes the impact of his Austin College experience: "The College, Sherman and its people unfolded the vision of life to me and there, ambition began to take a planned and tangible form. The old college and its faculty, with that close and individual touch, attainable only in the small college, exerted upon me as a youth, an influence which can never be dimmed. The associations there gave me friends and made a warm place in my heart for Sherman…"

Tec (left) with John Black (Tec's Best Man)

Tec was accepted at the University of Tennessee at Knoxville where he earned a bachelor of science degree in electrical engineering in 1900. He was athletic and played on the university's football team. After graduation, he continued his studies with courses at Massachusetts Institute of Technology.

Tec (left) and John Black

University of Tennessee 1899
(Tec: 3rd From left, 2nd Row from Top)

Tec began his electrical engineering career with the General Electric Company, training at its school in Lyon, Massachusetts. He was assigned as a supervisor when work on the Interurban line began and moved to McKinney where he met and married Katie Heard. He was an inventor and held the patent for the design of the original steam plant for McKinney.

When Tec and Katie moved to McKinney from Corpus Christi in 1911, Tec began his career as manager of the McKinney Compress. He also contracted his services as a consultant on many projects requiring an electrical engineer. He invested in real estate and insurance and managed most of the Heard family business after his father-in-law, Stephen, died in 1926. He was a partner in the Craig and Ray Insurance Company. Ray's granddaughter, Beverly Ray Scott, remembered him as a very kind and sweet gentleman who would give her a box of candy every Valentine's Day.

Tec was actively involved as an officer in the McKinney Chamber of Commerce, a member of the board of governors of the McKinney City Hospital for sixteen years (May 1929 - May 1945), and president of the Rotary Club. He held a directors position with the McKinney Ice and Coal Company, and the Collin County National Bank. He was a board member of several Dallas area firms: Gulf and Atlantic Insurance Company, Burrus Mills, Texas Textile Mill, and Fidelity Union Life Insurance Company. He was a member of the Texas Manufacturers Association, and actively participated as counselor and later as director in the East Texas Chamber of Commerce and Retail Credit Association.

Tec was a pioneer of scouting in McKinney. Boy Scouts of America began in 1910 and he started working with scouting in 1915, becoming a Scoutmaster and establishing McKinney's initial Boy Scout troop. Katie often served as a "den mother" before the scouting council created the position. She hiked with the group, cooked over an open fire, and is shown in a photo standing next to her pup tent wearing a Smokey the Bear hat. She went on nature trips collecting flowers, shells, and butterflies from her outdoor experiences. Tec received a Silver Beaver Award for distinguished service to young people within a local council, and a Bronze Star Award for twenty-five years of service from the area Circle Ten Council. In 1948, he was president and national representative of Circle Ten Boy Scouts of America. "This work he values next to his church and Christian education," notes Katie in a resume of his activities for Austin College. For many years, Tec presented each Eagle Scout in the area with a ring.

He served on the Austin College board of trustees for nearly a quarter of a century from 1934 until his death in 1957. He was one of "The Four Horsemen," a group of graduates and elders of the Presbyterian Church who sought support for the college at the Synod of the Presbyterian Church.

LIFE AT THE
HEARD-CRAIG HOME

On a typical day, Tec would have breakfast and then leave with his chauffeur to make the rounds – checking the rental properties and the cotton crops on their farms and then going to his insurance office. He used his engineering skills at home in his basement workshop, building an attic fan when he learned of the new concept, a single-seat elevator, intercom, and an automatic dog door for their beloved dog, Spoofer. Whenever Spoofer needed to go outside, he was trained to stand on a pad by the back door that would set off a buzzer. Even if Katie and Tec were upstairs they could push a button that would open the small door for Spoofer to go out.

Spoofer, Portrait by James Swann

Katie & Tec with Spoofer

Katie was a founder and charter member of the McKinney Art Club, established in 1914. The club members worked zealously to further art education in the community. She initiated one of the first statewide traveling art shows, bundling art herself and putting it on trains. When the artwork came back, she picked it up from the station and brought it to the public library for display. School children visited the library to see the artwork, and Katie gave lectures to them to enhance their appreciation of the art.

She was a member of the American Federation of Arts, and served twelve years as a trustee for the Texas Fine Arts Association. Katie co-wrote a fifty-year history of the McKinney Art Club. Always busy, she enjoyed china painting and was skilled at needlework. The social and civic whirl didn't keep her out of the garden, though. She often donned a hat, long- sleeved shirt, pants, and garden gloves to work amid her flowers throughout the spring and early summer.

She became a member of the Owl Club, a literary group, in 1934 at age fifty and often presented programs on art and other topics. In 1943, Owl Club programs focused

Art Club of McKinney (Katie standing, 1st on left)

Owl Club
(Katie seated, 4th from right)

on WWII efforts, with programs on national defense and the fourth meeting of each month dedicated to American Red Cross activities such as putting together surgical dressings.

When she died, the Owl Club noted in a resolution:

> "With great love and grief, the members of The Owl Club record the death of one of its dearest and most esteemed members, a person of keen mind, strong but gentle character, and far-reaching generosity - a useful and inspiring member of the Owl Club for thirty seven years, serving as president in 1944 - 45, and leaving a record through the years of loyalty, courage, and high ideals…"

A devout Presbyterian, Katie often walked to First Presbyterian Church when it was on Kentucky Street. In 1940, Tec was commissioner to the General Assembly of the Presbyterian Church USA from the Dallas Presbytery. He also served as deacon at the First Presbyterian Church. He had a direct line/intercom system installed from the church to Katie's bedroom so she could hear sermons when she was ill.

Katie suffered from poor health throughout her lifetime and hoped to find answers at the Mayo Clinic in the 1920s. A diagnosis was never confirmed, but her personal physician suggested that she spend time in a drier climate and take ten-minute sunbaths daily. This led to a great love of the American Southwest where they would travel often with Spoofer.

Katie and Tec would read to one another after dinner, his head in her lap as they shared classic books. Always devoted, Katie often referred to Tec as "the good man." Their greatest disappointment was that they were unable to have children of their own.

A FAMILY OF THEIR OWN

Hilda Thomas Truett remembers the day the Craigs came to visit the Itasca Orphanage, the Presbyterian home where she lived from age eight to eighteen. Katie was dressed up, and their chauffeur was in full uniform and cap. That February afternoon during the Great Depression, Hilda was drawing when Katie noticed her. When Katie asked her name, she learned it was the same as her best friend from college, who also liked to draw. They became fast friends and it wasn't long before the Craigs hoped to adopt her.

Hilda and her siblings had been placed in the orphanage after their mother was widowed and was unable to support them. Mrs. Thomas did not want her children to be adopted so the Craigs "unofficially" adopted Hilda. She "graduated" from the orphanage in 1935 and the Craigs helped secure a scholarship for her to attend Austin College where she would obtain a teaching certificate. Hilda said that people at college thought she was rich because of the beautiful clothes Katie made for her. She graduated from Austin College in 1938 and lived at the Craigs' home for a year while she taught sixth grade at North Ward Elementary School.

In the afternoons when she came home from teaching, Hilda would often find a board game set up on the floor and ready to play - Katie would have an activity organized for them to share. In the evenings when Hilda would come in from a date she and Katie would spend time talking about the date and share girl talk.

While living with the Craigs, Hilda began dating Luther Truett, a local attorney. Katie and Tec, concerned about Hilda's future, weren't convinced that Luther was the right choice. Being very astute and realizing their concern, Luther used the porch intercom to his advantage. Knowing that Tec would be listening to their conversation on the porch after a date, Luther would pay extravagant compliments to the Craigs.

He'd often say, "Hilda, you are the luckiest young woman in the world to have such wonderful people looking after you." It wasn't long before Tec was thoroughly convinced that Luther was the right man for Hilda and approved of their marriage, which took place on June 1, 1939.

It was the Craigs' great joy that the Truett children - Nancy, Jerry, and Katie (Katie Craig's namesake), became their grandchildren, calling them Granny and Grampy. The children fondly remember family gatherings, birthday parties, holidays, and Sunday dinners at the Craig's home. Their Granny baked birthday cakes, read to them, and played games with them. Katie was an expert seamstress and enjoyed making clothes for all of the family and the girls' dolls.

Craig & Truett Families Christmas 1952 (Sofa: Hilda, Nancy, Katie holding her namesake, Katie. Behind Sofa: Jerry, Luther, Tec)

Many of the most telling personal insights into Kathryn Heard Craig come from Jerry Truett. He and his mother, Hilda, paint a picture of a loving, devoted woman who was as kind as she was determined to improve education in McKinney. As Jerry notes, "A surrogate grandmother assumes that role out of love alone – not out of a sense of blood ties or bounden duty. She never aged as long as I knew her, the humorous twinkle never left her eye, the joie de vivre was her birthright."

She was formal, as were many women of that age and time, but she still loved a good game. Jerry still remembers a game of dominos that continued, unabated, while the tornado of 1948 blew through McKinney, destroying much of the town.

Jerry remembers rolling in the grass with Granny and Spoofer when he was around five. "She taught Spoofer and me valuable lessons," Truett writes. "Spoofer learned to be tolerant of others and to accept with magnanimity ear pullings and dental examinations from an inquisitive toddler. I began a lifelong love of animals." Adds Truett, "Never having had children of her own, she showered her mother's love on a multitude of us – in McKinney and beyond. Looking back, I stand in awe of the liberated woman's approach to life that Granny possessed."

"The Heard-Craig house itself was an impregnable fortress, an enchanted castle, a holy of holies and a maze of mysticism to a young boy, and I was no exception," according to Jerry. "Occasionally, about once a year, I was allowed to accompany Granny to the 'treasure room,' an upstairs screened-in porch. On those rare opportunities when the 'vault' was unlocked, Granny and I would sit for hours – the spellbinder and the spellbound. She'd show me the wonders of the chambered nautilus shell her father had given her as a child or the gigantic pine cone she and Grampy gathered in the Pacific Northwest."

Katie 1939

The neighbors' children also remembered coming to the Heard-Craig home and playing ball in the side yard. Five-year- old Brad Wysong and his brother lived across the street and would come over to toss the ball with her in the yard and play with Spoofer. Inside, they played hide and seek, and he remembers Katie showing them "a secret hideout" through a small door under the front stairs. Then there were cookies and lemonade served in crystal glasses in the dining room.

On Sundays there were formal family dinners with the Craigs and Truetts, filled with lots of laughter. During holiday meals the table was set with fine, tree-pattern china hand painted by Katie, fine linens, and silver place settings, plus individual salt and pepper shakers. A buzzer under the table could be pressed to alert the maid to bring the next course.

The Truett children enjoyed playing board games with Grampy in his room upstairs - where he kept a stash of candy and goodies on a shelf in his closet. He hid cans of sardines, small boxes of Limburger cheese, candy, and other treats the doctors had told him not to eat.

Nancy Truett Powell says that while her Granny was at times frail and in poor health, she was also a woman with "remarkable endurance, perseverance and courage to keep going and do what needed to be done as well as do what she wanted to do. She was very practical, very productive, very artistic, very kind, good and generous."

Katie Truett Martin recalls learning how to count at a very young age when Grampy told her that if she wanted to stay up with the adults she had to learn how to play dominoes. He taught her how to count by fives and tens as they played together.

Jerry also shared time together with Tec, in his basement workshop. He was meticulous with his tools, each of them outlined on the pegboard where they hung, down to the smallest drill bit. Jerry said:

"It was Grampy who gave me the inspiration to become a child Edison. When I was five, I concocted an idea for a mechanical fork that would facilitate the task of taking food from the plate to the mouth – thereby freeing both hands to do something more useful (like holding a Donald Duck funny book). I found a discarded electrical cord in the trash, Tinker Toys, some wire, and parts from an old alarm clock and made my apparatus. Knowing nothing of proper electrical grounding I plugged it into the wall. Kaboom – I was knocked across the room unconscious. When I revived, Mom and Dad were both glad I was still alive, or so they told me, but my experiment had blown out every fuse in our box and had knocked out the street lights and blown fuses at several of our neighbor's homes. Granny took me in her arms and led me to Grampy. She required him to teach me the world of electricity - the world of men - and he did, too."

KATHRYN HEARD CRAIG
BUSINESSWOMAN AND
COLLEGE TRUSTEE

In a letter to a Craig family member, Katie described her daily life in 1950:

> These past few years I have given much of my time and effort to assisting with the business. And since we have most of these transactions here at home, I never know when the doorbell or phone will interrupt me. I also keep the cash or receipt book, type letters for Tec, and I am learning somewhat about other bookkeeping, all this in addition to my other duties of running the home and looking after Tec when he is not feeling well. He gets blue at times and wants me to entertain him, which I often do by reading aloud to him.

Instead of reading the classics aloud to Tec, she chose The Wall Street Journal, and kept an eye on other financial publications as well. She was tutored by Tec and was well into management of family interests by the time of his death from a stroke on March 28, 1957, at age eighty-two.

Katie was appointed to fill her husband's position on the Austin College Board of Trustees. She began an education in the world of college finance and management. She immediately requested the board's by-laws, studied them and took a self-evaluation test for College Board members. Before her first board meeting, she included these thoughts in a letter to Austin College President Dr. John D. Moseley: "I do hope and pray that I, as a member of the board, may prove to be of some real service to the College and in some way helpful to the Board. Am looking forward to the Board meeting in Fort Worth, but of course, it will be a sad one for me without my beloved, who for so many years never missed a meeting."

She would invite Dr. Moseley to her home, where she would be waiting with a long list of questions. Katie would drill him on previous issues and future projects. "It was like the Hour of Parliament, she had her notes, her questions and had read everything I had sent her as trustee," said the late Dr. Moseley, president emeritus. "I enjoyed that, as it was really a concern for the college in the best sense of the word."

Her concern for higher education also extended to her alma mater, Mary Baldwin College. She made contributions annually and established the Katie Florence Heard Craig Scholarship in 1957, which is still awarded. In January 1964, she specified that a portion of the funds she had given to an endowment be set aside and earmarked for the building of a Science Center.

She returned to Mary Baldwin with her cousin Bessie and niece, Dale, in 1960 to hear President Dwight D. Eisenhower speak. It was her first flight, and she wrote, "The cloud formations on return were heavenly in their beauty."

This was the only time she would return to campus, although she was invited to come in 1964 to receive the Algernon Sydney Sullivan Medallion award. The award is still presented annually "as a permanent reminder of the noblest human qualities and for unselfish service to their alma mater and the community at large." Having been in and out of the hospital during that year, she was unable to make the trip. Professor John B. Daffin accepted the award in her absence from the college's President, Dr. Spencer. The citation stated that she had shown "a devotion to Christian education which parallels that of Rufus Bailey," founder of Mary Baldwin College.

President Moseley received notes from Katie on stocks she gave the college, detailing upward or downward trends and enclosing newspaper clippings to substantiate her findings. Often she would discuss other financial news she read in Capital Advisors, Inc. as well as The Wall Street Journal. She was conversant on economic theories, market analysis, government spending policy, and foreign affairs.

She was re-elected to the Austin College Board after she completed her husband's term, and was a trustee until 1964. In memory of Tec, she helped fund a music building on campus that was dedicated on April 28, 1962. The new Craig Hall Music Building featured a theater workshop, a lecture and rehearsal hall, a sculpture court, offices, and classrooms. The second floor offered rooms for design, drawing, painting, artists' studios, print and slide study, film storage, art department offices, the chairman's office, an eight-foot wide exhibit gallery and a ten-foot wide exhibit gallery.

The college commissioned portraits of Katie and Tec to hang in Craig Hall. Katie questioned the need for such an expense, noting "…I am not fully convinced that at this time other things may not be more necessary." She pointed out that other families had given buildings to the college without portraits of themselves.

Katie's vision of her role as trustee encompassed an interest in the whole college. As a board member she believed in coming to the campus between board meetings and visiting with students, faculty, and administration "to get a better idea of what is really happening on the campus - what is taught and how, ensuring teachers and students are happy in their work. . ."

A letter sent to Dr. Moseley in 1964 revealed her as a woman ahead of her time when she inquired about the curriculum for math majors, noting that "they will be very much in demand as operators of electronic computers."

Tec

Thomas Edgar Craig - Craig Hall Portrait

In the spring of 1970, Austin College announced additions to Craig Hall, stating that they were funded by Mrs. Kathryn Heard Craig. She was appalled to find this information detailing even her home address in the papers. As always, Katie requested the college be very discreet in their announcements when referring to her philanthropic efforts.

Kathryn Heard Craig- Craig Hall Portrait

She preferred no mention of her name at all. Katie's focus on giving is evident from a letter she wrote to Dr. Moseley on April 16, 1970, just eight months before she died:

> ...I do hope that Craig Hall will continue to be a real help in the Lord's work, teaching young people sacred music, how beautiful it can be, and helpful in so many different ways and places. In addition, that the new wing for painting and other

arts will prove as helpful to the Church and Community in other ways of teaching the beauty of Christianity. I pray that all who go through its halls and classes will come out better men and women and whatever calling they may pursue in life, their light will shine brightly pointing others to the value of a truly Christ-oriented college as I hope and believe Austin College to be. Such colleges are greatly needed in these trying times…

The addition included a new Art Wing, a two-story wing to the east entrance to match the west wing. It also placed on the north a one-story rehearsal room addition near the entrance to the Craig Hall Recital Room.

The text of the Art Wing plaque reads:

The Art Wing was given by Mrs. Kathryn Heard Craig as further evidence of her affection for Austin College and support of the arts. The Board of Trustees of Austin College honors the memory of Kathryn Heard Craig, whose devotion as a trustee and whose major request makes possible the continued educational leadership of Austin College.

Katie made Austin College scholarships for tuition available for the children of several McKinney families, in addition to four endowments established by the Heard and Craig families at Austin College:

- Endowed by Mr. and Mrs. S. D. Heard (Katie's parents): The S. D. Heard Fellowship of English by Mr. and Mrs. S. D. Heard in 1925
- Endowed by Mr. and Mrs. Thomas E. Craig: The Thomas Edgar and Kathryn Heard Craig Fellowship in Business Administration and Economics in 1953

- Endowed by Mrs. Kathryn Heard Craig: The Stephen Dudley and Lillie S. Heard Fellowship in Science in 1960
- Endowed through the Thomas E. Craig, Stephen Dudley Heard, and Lillie D. Heard Memorial Trust established by Mrs. Kathryn Heard Craig in memory of her husband and parents in 1970: The Craig Professorship in the Arts

Through her will, Katie provided for six charities: Austin College; First Presbyterian Church, McKinney; Heard-Craig Woman's Club Trust (d.b.a. Heard-Craig Center for the Arts); Itasca Orphanage; Pan American School; and Presbyterian Village. She also provided for seven individuals: her niece, Dale Heard Lambert; Hilda Thomas Truett; two of Mr. Craig's nieces; two cousins; and her housekeeper, Edna McKenzie.

Kathryn Heard Craig died at 8:45 a.m. on Wednesday, December 9, 1970, at Collin Memorial Hospital in McKinney after a long battle with breast cancer. She was buried next to Tec in the Heard family plot at Pecan Grove Cemetery in McKinney.

Kathryn Heard Craig and her husband were two of McKinney's greatest community leaders and supporters. Their philanthropy and untold hours of service left an indelible mark on the city.

BESSIE ROLLINS HEARD (1886 – 1988)

Bessie Rollins Heard, the eldest daughter of John and Rachel Heard, was known affectionately as Miss Bess. She was the first girl to ride a bicycle in McKinney at the turn of the century, which prompted her grandmother to comment that it was "most undignified for a young girl." She was bold, outspoken, and independent throughout her long life. Asked about her early life she said, "I was a tomboy as a child and spent a lot of time horseback riding and watching the birds, animals, and trees."

Bessie Heard

Bessie

She often said that it was her sister, Laura, who was an accomplished musician, but her father thought that all his girls should receive musical training. "I took lessons on the violin at one time, but I didn't get very far. I played at only one recital held in the Heard Opera House, which was probably sufficient to convince my teacher and father not to waste any more time on me."

In 1902, Bessie, her sister, Nina, and cousin, Katie, attended school together at Mary Baldwin Seminary (College) in Staunton, Virginia through 1905. It was common then to send girls back East for training and education.

Bessie

Bessie toured Canada and Europe in 1913 with her sister, Laura, and six other young women who were chaperoned by Miss Ona Brown. The trip included a visit to Ireland, homeland of the Heard ancestors. She remarked on the beauty of the country and how much she enjoyed riding horses through the countryside. A McKinney Courier Gazette article in October 1979 quoted her as saying, "I recall that Miss Brown would review each of us each night on the day's activities to see how much we had learned." With a twinkle in her eye she added, "After all, this trip was supposed to be for educational purposes." A highlight of the trip was a stop in Paris where the girls had couture gowns made for them.

Ireland 1913
(Laura: 1st from left, Bess: back row, 1st from right)

Inspired by a great love of nature, Bessie organized a bird-house contest in 1916 for neighborhood children, to teach them how to feed and care for birds. Later the same year she began a beautification of the McKinney town square by selecting and planting hackberry trees.

She moved to New York City in 1916 to study interior design at Parson's School of Design. Returning to Texas, she accepted a position as an interior decorator with Halaby's Galleries (later a part of Neiman Marcus) in Dallas. When her parents' health declined, she resigned her position and moved back to McKinney to help her sisters with their care.

1916 Birdhouse Contest

Bessie – Class Assignment, Parsons

Brewster Ranch, Edmonton, Canada 1925 (l: Laura, Bessie)

During World War I, Bessie was instrumental in establishing a local American Red Cross, and served as a "Gray Lady" volunteer. She and other volunteers spent hours in the hot coliseum, sewing bandages for the war effort. She focused considerable energy in 1937 on raising funds to build a much-needed library, and was a lifelong benefactor.

A self-described "packrat," Bessie had an extensive collection of seashells and butterflies that she delighted in showing to area children. "I may have some real duds in my collection, but I love them all," she told a local reporter. Her collections included original prints by Audubon and Redoute, oriental art and artifacts, and nature related knick-knacks. She loved to shop for hats and had a large collection suitable for any occasion.

Bessie
(2nd from Right)

Ashburn General Hospital, McKinney 1944
(Bessie: 1st on left, Artist, Frank Klepper, 1st on Right)

Bessie said that she was too choosy to get married, but that as a single woman she lived a very free and independent life. When asked how she would be remembered she said, "Oh, I don't know. When you're gone, you're gone."

As Bessie witnessed the continued growth of McKinney, she grew concerned because so much of the land was being developed. At the age of seventy-eight, at a time when most would be content to look back over their lifetime, she began to consider building a museum. Her vision was to build a museum to house her many collections and to preserve a portion of Collin County as open space for future generations to enjoy.

Bessie Heard- 1945
Sheppard Field, Wichita Falls, Texas

Dr. Harold Laughlin, hand chosen by Miss Bess to be the museum's first director, told of meeting in her home where she would plop down on the floor and unroll the many blueprints of her museum building. She would point out the exhibit halls and share her vision for the future when an expansion would include a planetarium. Laughlin said that once the museum was under construction, she would drive herself to the site and "climb down an old, rickety ladder despite having vertigo and a detached retina. There wasn't anything she wouldn't try."

Her dream, the Heard Natural Science Museum & Wildlife Sanctuary, opened its doors on October 1, 1967. In a 1969 interview Miss Bess said, "This country will be covered over with concrete before long at the rate they're bulldozing everything down. I wanted to save a portion of Collin County land with its native vegetation and wildlife before it gets plowed under."

In keeping with Miss Heard's vision, the museum's mission is threefold: education, conservation, and preservation. Through education, particularly for young people, the Heard Natural Science Museum emphasizes an appreciation of nature and its conservation.

When interviewed at age eighty-three, Miss Bess said that her traveling days were almost over, but not quite. "I can't drive as much as I used to and that cramps my style," she said with a little smile. Miss Bess passed away just two months shy of her 102nd birthday.

NINA HEARD ASTIN (1888 - 1972)
ROGER Q. ASTIN (1887 – 1926)

Nina Stigler Heard Astin attended Mary Baldwin Seminary (College) with sister Bessie and cousin Kathryn from 1902 - 1905. She married Roger Q. Astin on January 20, 1909, and lived in his hometown of Bryan, Texas. Roger Q. Astin was the son of wealthy parents and was known as a "gentleman" farmer and planter. Nina and Roger were the parents of three children: John Heard Astin (1910 – 1958), Nina Bess Astin Winkler (1914 – 1967), and Daisy Caroline Astin (1921 – 1923).

Nina Heard Astin

Roger Q. Astin

Nina with her children, Nina Bess and John

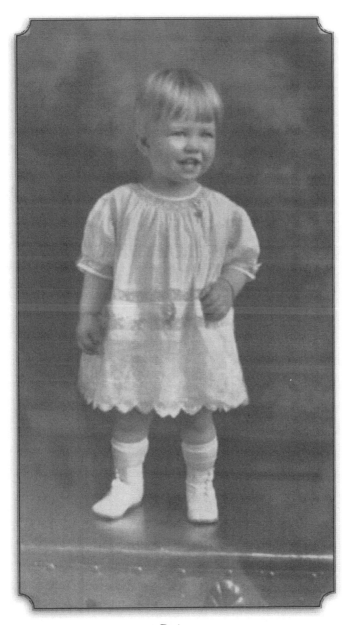

Daisy

Astin Home- Built 1921

The Astins lived in the plantation home built by Roger's parents prior to building their own beautiful home. An animal lover like her sisters, Nina, once described her new home as "a mansion with dog kennels." She raised canaries to sell in McKinney in the building her father leased to F. W. Woolworth. Nina, like her mother, Rachel, loved to do handwork and made many quilts.

Nina's strong faith and her dedication to the Presbyterian Church helped her live through the tragedies in her life. Daughter Daisy died from a kidney disorder before reaching her second birthday in 1923. Her husband, Roger, died at the age of thirty-eight in 1926 after being struck by a train. Nina outlived her son, John Heard Astin, who was forty-eight when he died; and daughter, Nina Bess Astin Winkler who died at age fifty-three. Both of their deaths were from lung cancer.

Nina remained in Bryan though she was a regular visitor to her family in McKinney. She continued her family's legacy of giving and was a benefactor of Texas A&M University. Just before her death she dedicated a park, the Astin Recreation Area. The Nina Heard Astin Trust has funded many civic and cultural projects in the city of Bryan and continues to do so today.

LAURA HEARD SHOAP (1893 – 1971)
HENRY SHOAP (1899 – 1977)

Laura Evlyn Heard Shoap, the youngest of John and Rachel Heard's daughters, was outgoing and enjoyed being around people. She was an excellent musician who played organ and piano at First Presbyterian Church where she was a lifetime member. An accomplished violinist, she gave numerous recitals at the Heard Opera House.

Laura

Laura

She attended Texas Presbyterian College in Milford and played on the basketball team. She married McKinney businessman Henry Shoap, owner of the local Royal Crown Bottling Company of McKinney on February 25, 1939, at age forty-five. The plant was located on property where Laura's grandfather, Charles Clarkston Heard, operated the City Hotel.

Henry was described as a perfect gentleman and Laura as a perfect lady. Laura was an astute businesswoman and

Laura

took over the responsibility of her father's business affairs after her parents died. She also directed the John S. and Rachel Heard Foundation.

Although she had no children of her own she was active with the children's music ministry of her church. Laura's sister, Bessie, said that Laura dearly loved children and children loved her. When she walked into a room the children would flock to her immediately.

The Shoaps were strong proponents of the value of education. They were instrumental in establishing the McKinney Education Foundation with their initial donation of 1.2 million dollars. Named for her parents, the John S. and Rachel Heard Scholarship is awarded each year to students with proven academic achievement, community and school involvement, and leadership abilities. The Shoaps contributed $50,000 in 1963 to Austin College - to remodel Luckett Hall on campus, and to establish and partly endow the Henry L. and Laura H. Shoap Professorship of English.

Laura and Henry established a Shoap Boys Club that evolved into the current McKinney branch of the Boys & Girls Club of Collin County. They made generous contributions to the local hospital for equipment and nurses training.

Miss Bess, Laura, and her husband, Henry Shoap, shared the family's residence built by their parents in 1921 on North College Street. The Shoaps lived on one floor with Bess on the other floor.

J. S. Heard Home
Built by John C Rachel Heard

THE HEARD-CRAIG
CENTER FOR THE ARTS

Kathryn Heard Craig was a visionary and she was so convinced of the power of women's clubs for women individually and for the community that she conceived of the idea of the Heard-Craig Woman's Club Trust in 1955. It was her wish that upon her death, her family home would become a "club house" for use by the women's clubs of McKinney. She felt that if she could provide a permanent meeting place for the women's clubs that they would continue to flourish and provide immeasurable opportunities for their members.

The women of Katie's generation, growing up in the late 1800s, had limited educational opportunities. It was unusual for most of these women to have the opportunity to attend college. Katie was fortunate to have parents who believed that women should be educated.

Most of the women of the Heard girls' generation joined the women's clubs of the time in order to further their education. The clubs were based on the study programs of the Chautauqua Institute in Chautauqua, New York. Their purpose was primarily educational or literary in nature. Many of the clubs soon became involved in programs for community improvement. The women raised money to build libraries, provided schools with books, and completed civic beautification projects. By 1915, more than three million women were club members. The clubs have not only enhanced their communities through service projects, but they have also enhanced the lives of American women by providing educational enlightenment, social camaraderie, and a greater sense of self-worth and achievement.

Katie's dream was to provide a facility that would encourage the "education and enlightenment" of women and appreciation of the arts. She carefully planned for the establishment of the Heard-Craig Woman's Club Trust, the organization that would go into effect upon her death.

When she passed away in 1970, the seven women who would form the first board of trustees had already been appointed. The organization received non-profit status from the Internal Revenue Service on August 24, 1971. Since that time thousands of women have used the facilities for education, fellowship, and civic benevolence. There are twenty clubs and groups still meeting in the facilities with more than 32,000 guests attending events throughout the year.

The Heard-Craig celebrated forty years of service to women and the community in August 2011. The success of the organization has been possible because of the guidance of an exceptional group of trustees and dedicated staff members during the past forty years. This success has only been possible because of the brilliance, generosity, and vision of a remarkable woman, Kathryn Heard Craig.

Heard-Craig House
Built by Stephen & Lillie Heard

Made in the USA
Columbia, SC
01 September 2024

40945216R00071